LAYERS OF STONE

HOW

EARTH'S BIGGEST CAVES

FORMED

DANIEL R. FAUST

PowerKiDS
press

New York

Published in 2020 by The Rosen Publishing Group, Inc.
29 East 21st Street, New York, NY 10010

First Edition

Editor: Sarah Machajewski
Book Design: Tanya Dellaccio

Photo Credits: Cover Boon Tang/500px Prime/Getty Images; p. 5 Anirut Thailand/Shutterstock.com; p. 7 (top) Webspark/Shutterstock.com; p. 7 (bottom) Leene/Shutterstock.com; p. 9 3xy/Shutterstock.com; p. 11 Amineah/Shutterstock.com; p. 13 (top) Wangkun Jia/Shutterstock.com; pp. 13 (bottom), 25 Vietnam Stock Images/Shutterstock.com; p. 14 annie_zhak/Shutterstock.com; p. 15 FCG/Shutterstock.com; p. 17 Lucia Terui/Moment/Getty Images; p. 18 Ralf Lehmann/Shutterstock.com; p. 19 Robin Runck/Shutterstock.com; p. 21 J. Helgason/Shutterstock.com; p. 22 Armando Frazao/Shutterstock.com; p. 23 MATJAZ SLANIC/E+/Getty Images; p. 27 Marco Barone/Shutterstock.com; p. 29 Xinhua News Agency/Getty Images; p. 30 Piotr Krzeslak/Shutterstock.com.

Library of Congress Cataloging-in-Publication Data

Names: Faust, Daniel R., author.
Title: Layers of stone : how Earth's biggest caves formed / Daniel R. Faust.
Description: New York : PowerKids Press, [2020] | Series: Earth's history
  through rocks | Includes index.
Identifiers: LCCN 2018053246| ISBN 9781725301528 (pbk.) | ISBN 9781725301542
  (library bound) | ISBN 9781725301535 (6 pack)
Subjects: LCSH: Caves-Juvenile literature. | Speleology-Juvenile
  literature. | Geology, Structural-Juvenile literature. |
  Landforms-Juvenile literature.
Classification: LCC GB601.2 .F3855 2020 | DDC 551.44/7-dc23
LC record available at https://lccn.loc.gov/2018053246

Manufactured in the United States of America

CPSIA Compliance Information: Batch #CSPK19. For Further Information contact Rosen Publishing, New York, New York at 1-800-237-9932.

CONTENTS

NOT JUST SOME HOLE IN THE GROUND

When you're walking down the street or hanging out with your friends at the park, you probably think you're standing on solid ground. The ground beneath your feet feels pretty firm, doesn't it? It might surprise you to learn that the ground is full of holes.

Many of these holes are man-made. There are holes in the ground that contain pipes that carry water to and from our homes. Others hold cables and wires that deliver electricity and other services. Some holes are made by the natural processes of the earth. These holes are called caves. Caves are large, hollow places that have been carved into rock by wind, water, and other forces.

CAVE OR CAVERN?

Sometimes people think they can use the words "cave" and "cavern" to describe the same thing, but there's a difference. A cave is any opening in the ground large enough that part of it isn't exposed to direct sunlight. A cavern is a type of cave that's formed when water soaks into the ground and affects a specific type of rock.

A well is a kind of man-made hole. People dig wells deep into the ground to provide communities with clean drinking water.

LAYERS EVERYWHERE

Earth has four main layers. At the center of the planet is the inner core, which is a mass of solid iron and nickel. Around the inner core is a layer of hot liquid metal known as the outer core. The core layers are surrounded by a shell of solid and semisolid rock called the mantle. The outermost layer of the earth is called the crust. The crust includes everything we see on the surface of the planet, such as ocean beds and mountains.

In addition to the four layers that make up Earth, the crust itself is made of different layers. These layers, or strata, are made of different kinds of rock, soil, and minerals. The different layers that make up the crust are where caves form.

Each band of color in this rock formation represents a different kind of substance. Scientists study the strata found in rocks to learn about Earth's past. ▶

CRUST
MANTLE
OUTER CORE
INNER CORE

READING THE ROCKS

EARTH'S LITHOSPHERE, WHICH INCLUDES THE CRUST AND PART OF THE UPPER MANTLE, IS BROKEN INTO LARGE PIECES CALLED TECTONIC PLATES. THE MOVEMENT OF THESE PLATES CREATES MOUNTAINS AND CAUSES VOLCANOES AND EARTHQUAKES.

WATER ON THE ROCKS

Let's take a closer look at the processes that form caves. Caves can be formed by chemical **reactions** and physical reactions. However they're formed, water is a key part of the process.

The water cycle is the ongoing movement of water on, above, and beneath the surface of the earth. Water changes as it moves through different phases, or stages. Water **evaporates** from Earth's surface and rises as water vapor. It cools in the clouds, turning back into liquid water. This water returns to the surface in the form of **precipitation** such as rain or snow. Water that doesn't flow back into the world's oceans, rivers, and lakes soaks into the ground. The water seeps in and interacts with the soil and stone that make up Earth's surface.

We might not be able to see all the phases of the water cycle, but the process is going on all around us. ▶

THE WATER CYCLE

HEAT FROM THE SUN TURNS LIQUID WATER INTO WATER VAPOR, WHICH RISES INTO THE AIR.

THE WATER VAPOR COOLS AND TURNS BACK INTO LIQUID WATER, FORMING CLOUDS.

WATER FALLS FROM THE SKY IN THE FORM OF RAIN, SNOW, HAIL, OR SLEET.

CONDENSATION

PRECIPITATION

EVAPORATION

COLLECTION

PRECIPITATION COLLECTS IN LAKES, RIVERS, AND OCEANS. MUCH PRECIPITATION SOAKS INTO THE GROUND.

9

As water falls to Earth, it can pick up **contaminants** from air pollution, which can change how water reacts with certain kinds of rock. The water in rivers and other waterways can wear away at rock and stone to create valleys and canyons, such as the Grand Canyon. The movement of the oceans creates and changes the shape of the coastlines.

Water that seeps into the ground can also change the shape of Earth's landscapes. This water creates caves. Just like the way rivers and oceans can **erode** rock and stone on Earth's surface, water can **dissolve** certain kinds of substances found inside the earth. When the water level **recedes**, it leaves behind hollow chambers in the solid stone.

The Grand Canyon is just one example of the effect moving water can have on Earth's surface. This natural wonder was created by millions of years of erosion by the Colorado River.

You may be lucky enough to live in an area where there are caves to explore, but these caves are probably not that big. However, there are some truly massive caves around the world. In Vietnam, a drop of more than 200 feet (61 m) takes explorers into the Son Doong Cave, which is over 5.5 miles (8.9 km) long.

The Mulu Caves on the island of Borneo are home to the largest cave chamber. This chamber is longer than 2,000 feet (609.6 m) and more than 260 feet (79.3 m) high. That's large enough to hold 40 airplanes! The Sistema Sac Actun in Mexico is the second-longest underwater cave system in the world. Only 130 miles (209.2 km) of it have been explored. The cave is a popular destination for snorkelers and scuba divers.

READING THE ROCKS

A COLLAPSED ROOF IN THE SON DOONG CAVE ALLOWS IN ENOUGH SUNLIGHT FOR PLANTS TO GROW. IN THE CHAMBER'S "UNDERGROUND JUNGLE," SOME TREES ARE 100 FEET (30.5 M) TALL.

At more than 400 miles (643.7 km) long, Mammoth Cave in Kentucky is the world's longest cave system. Visitors to Mammoth Cave can see unique plants and animals and beautiful cave formations.

SON DOONG CAVE

WHAT A DRIP

There are different kinds of caves, and each kind is formed through a different process. When you think of a cave, the kind you picture is most likely a solutional cave. The chemical processes that create solutional caves work because of the different layers of material within Earth's crust.

In places where there's a layer of soil on top of a layer of limestone or a similar type of stone, water can seep through the soil and into cracks in the stone. As the water moves through the soil, it picks up carbon dioxide and forms a weak solution, or mixture, of carbonic acid, which dissolves the limestone. Over time, as more water drains through the soil, this solution of carbonic acid dissolves enough limestone to create a cave.

Many common features of solutional caves, such as stalactites and stalagmites, are a result of the dripping water that formed the cave.

CATCH A WAVE

Another type of cave is a sea cave. As the name suggests, sea caves can be found along the coastlines of large bodies of water such as oceans and lakes. Sea caves are formed by the constant motion of waves as they crash against the shore. These waves contain sand and gravel. The motion of the waves grinds these small **particles** against the rock and stone of the coastline, slowly eroding it over time.

Sea caves are an excellent example of the power that water has to change the shape of Earth's surface. Studying sea caves and understanding how water interacts with the coastline are becoming increasingly important as sea levels continue to rise and coastal erosion becomes more common.

READING THE ROCKS

THE AVERAGE SEA CAVE IS USUALLY BETWEEN 16 AND 164 FEET (4.9 AND 50 M) LONG, BUT SOME CAN BE AS LONG AS 980 FEET (298.7 M).

Sometimes the pressure from the waves that create sea caves is so great that it forces the water up to the cave ceiling, where it creates another opening called a blowhole.

LET IT FLOW

Magma is liquid or semiliquid rock that exists beneath Earth's crust. When magma erupts or creeps from cracks in Earth's surface, we call it lava. When lava cools, it forms new geological features such as volcanoes, domes, and even entire islands. Lava can also form caves.

A lava flow is a moving mass of lava. As a lava flow moves, the outer layer begins to cool and harden, forming igneous rock. Even though the outermost layer is now solid stone, the liquid lava continues to flow beneath it. When the lava flows away, a hollow tube beneath a layer of stone remains. This is called a lava tube, lava cave, or primary cave. Many of the caves found on the islands of Hawaii are lava caves.

Because they're formed from rock that comes from deep inside Earth, lava tubes are an excellent way for scientists to get a glimpse of our planet's interior.

ICE TO MEET YOU

A glacier is a large mass of slow-moving ice. Glaciers are found all over the world. Because of their size and weight, moving glaciers change the shape of Earth's surface. Glaciers can create valleys, lakes, and many other geological features. A glacier can also form caves within the glacier itself.

Like solutional caves and sea caves, glacier caves are formed by water moving through or against mostly solid material. As ice on the surface of the glacier melts, the water can drain into cracks and **fissures** in the ice. This water is warmer than the surrounding ice, so some ice begins to melt, which causes the cracks to grow. This process creates tubelike shafts that run up and down the height of the glacier.

READING THE ROCKS

AS A GLACIER MOVES, IT PICKS UP LARGE PIECES OF ROCK AND CARRIES THEM TO OTHER PLACES, SOMETIMES AS FAR AS A FEW HUNDRED MILES. THESE CHUNKS OF ROCK ARE CALLED GLACIAL ERRATICS.

Some glaciers appear to be blue because the ice absorbs red and yellow light and only lets the blue light pass through.

DEPOSITS, COLUMNS, AND CLIMATE

Perhaps the most fascinating thing about caves is the unique physical formations that we can find within them. These columns, mounds, and tubes not only illustrate how caves are formed, but they can hold valuable data about how Earth's climate is changing.

"Speleothem" is the scientific name for these formations, but they're more commonly called cave deposits. Speleothems come in many different shapes and sizes. Flowstone is sheetlike and can be found on the walls and floors of caves. It's created when running water deposits minerals on the walls or floor of a cave. Mineral deposits are also responsible for the creation of cave crystals, such as dogtooth spars.

DOGTOOTH SPARS

BATS ALL, FOLKS!

There are more than 1,200 species of bats in the world, and they have an important role in a balanced environment. Many bats eat insects, which helps agriculture. The more insects eaten by bats, the fewer there are to ruin crops. Some bats also help to pollinate plants. Many bats live in caves, so protecting caves also protects bats. If we destroy the bats' homes, we'll be hurting ourselves too.

Caves can be wondrous places full of breathtaking rock formations and strange creatures such as the olm salamander. The olm salamander is one of the few amphibian species that can live in total darkness.

Dripstones might be the most well-known cave deposits. Stalactites are the pointy formations that hang from cave ceilings. Stalagmites are similar to stalactites, but they grow up from the ground rather than down from the ceiling. Columns are cave deposits that form when a stalactite and a stalagmite meet. Some columns are formed when a stalactite grows long enough to touch the floor of the cave on its own.

Cave deposits are more than just something pretty to look at. Scientists can study these formations to learn about environmental conditions. Temperature, **humidity**, and annual rainfall can all affect the formation of cave deposits. Studying the elements found in these formations can help scientists figure out what Earth's climate was like in the past.

Cave pearls, like those pictured here, start off as tiny particles inside a cave pool. The particles get coated in a layer of calcite. Over time, layers and layers of calcite create "pearl" forms. ▶

SPELEOTHEMS: KNOW THE LINGO

Stalactites: Pointed structures that hang from cave ceilings.

Soda straws: Very long, thin stalactites.

Stalagmites: The mound-like growths on a cave floor.

Helictites: Twisty shapes that form on cave ceilings, walls, and floors.

Curtains: Thin, wavy sheetlike growths.

Shelfstones: Structures that grow inward from a cave pool.

Cave pearls: Sphere-shaped deposits that form in cave pools. They aren't attached to surfaces.

Anthodites: Flowerlike clusters of crystal.

CAVE PEARLS

WHAT'S A SPELUNKER?

The Latin word for "cave" is "spelunca." The English words "spelunker" and "speleologist" both come from that word. A spelunker is someone whose hobby is studying and exploring caves and cave networks. A speleologist is a scientist who studies caves and cave networks as their job.

Some people explore caves for fun. Spelunkers, or cavers, enjoy exploring cave networks and discovering new caves. In addition to the exercise, many spelunkers are drawn to the activity because they can **survey** and map unexplored caves. Although the activity is fun, cavers must be serious about personal safety and protecting caves. Additionally, cavers know to never enter a cave alone and to never go spelunking without telling others.

Exploring caves can be dangerous. It's important that you have the right kind of equipment, multiple light sources, and plenty of drinking water. ▶

READING THE ROCKS

THE NATIONAL SPELEOLOGICAL SOCIETY WAS FORMED BY AMERICAN SPELUNKERS IN 1941. THE ORGANIZATION'S GOAL IS TO ADVANCE EXPLORATION, CONSERVATION, STUDY, AND UNDERSTANDING OF CAVES IN THE UNITED STATES.

Speleologists devote their lives to studying different aspects of the **ecosystems** located within caves. Speleologists study the geological processes that form caves, including the movement of water. They also study the different kinds of plants and animals that call a cave network home. Speleologists also survey caves in order to develop maps of a cave network.

Whether explorer or scientist, anyone who spends enough time surrounded by the underground wonders of Earth's caves and caverns knows how important it is to protect them. Major changes in climate threaten caves, and the disappearance of plant and animals species that rely on caves harms their ecosystems.

THAILAND CAVE RESCUE

On June 23, 2018, a soccer team of 12 boys and their coach were trapped in the Tham Luang caves of Thailand's Chiang Rai province. The caves were a familiar exploration site, but recent rains had made them dangerous. The boys and their coach became trapped as the caves flooded with water. After two weeks and a global rescue effort, all 13 were rescued unharmed.

In October 2018, a massive cave system was discovered at the bottom of a sinkhole much like this one. Scientists hope the cave, located in China's Guangxi forest, can teach us more about Earth's past.

SAVING CAVES

Many people probably think of caves as just dark holes in the ground. Maybe you're curious about what you might find there. Whether or not you think caves might be a fun place to explore, it's important to remember that caves are also ecosystems.

Caves are home to countless species of plants and animals. If caves are destroyed, these living things could die out. Also, the unique formations found in many caves take thousands of years to form. If they're damaged or destroyed, they might never be replaced. The most important thing any cave explorer can do is remember to never damage or remove anything they find in a cave.

GLOSSARY

contaminant: Something that contaminates, or pollutes, another substance.

dissolve: To break down a solid when a liquid mixes with that solid.

ecosystem: A natural community of living and nonliving things.

erode: To wear away something by natural forces.

evaporate: To change from a liquid into a gas.

fissure: A narrow opening or crack, such as in rocks or the earth's crust.

humidity: The amount of moisture in the air.

particle: A very small piece of something.

precipitation: Water that falls to the ground as hail, mist, rain, sleet, or snow.

reaction: Something that happens because of something else.

recede: To slowly move back.

survey: To measure and examine an area of land.

INDEX

WEBSITES

Due to the changing nature of Internet links, PowerKids Press has developed an online list of websites related to the subject of this book. This site is updated regularly. Please use this link to access the list: www.powerkidslinks.com/EHTR/caves

TITLES IN THIS SERIES

THE HIGHEST PEAK
HOW MOUNT EVEREST FORMED

LAVA AND MAGMA
HOW THE HAWAIIAN ISLANDS FORMED

LAYERS OF STONE
HOW EARTH'S BIGGEST CAVES FORMED

MOVING ICE
HOW THE GREAT LAKES FORMED

REEFS AND VOLCANOES
HOW EARTH'S ATOLLS FORMED

WATER AND ROCK
HOW THE GRAND CANYON FORMED

GRL: T

ISBN: 9781725301528
6-pack ISBN: 9781725301535

9 781725 301528

PowerKiDS
press